Abraham
Man of Faith

ELSIE RIVES • ILLUSTRATED BY **WILLIAM N. McPHEETERS**

BROADMAN PRESS
Nashville, Tennessee

© Copyright 1976 ● Broadman Press
All rights reserved
4242-23
ISBN: 0-8054-4223-5

Dewey Decimal Classification: J 221.92
Subject heading: ABRAHAM
Printed in the United States of America

Contents

A Trip Without a Map

In the city of Ur a large crowd of people were marching in the streets. A long ago New Year's celebration had begun. In the procession, men carried on their shoulders the golden idol of the moon-god, Nannar-Sin. They were going to the place of worship at the high tower of the ziggurat.

Ur was a beautiful city located near the Euphrates and Tigris rivers. Here most of the people prayed and bowed down to idols of the moon, the sun, and the stars. They were wise and smart people. Canals were dug to bring water from the river into all parts of the city and to the fertile lands nearby. In the schools boys were taught reading, writing, and numbers. They wrote on clay tablets. Craftsmen of the city made beautiful pottery and other objects of gold and clay. Ur was an old and important city four thousand years ago.

5

In this place between the rivers lived a man named Abram. He was not like the other people of the city. He did not worship the idol gods. He believed in only one God, the true God who made the earth, the people, and all things.

Abram lived with Terah, his father, Nahor and Haran, his brothers, Sarai, his wife and Lot, a nephew. The family owned many sheep, goats, and cattle. They probably lived outside the city near the rich pasture land so

that their herds of animals could find food
and water. Abram and his family were
nomads and herdsmen.

Although Abram did not know it, God had
a special plan for all the world. He needed
Abram to help him with this plan.

One day God spoke to Abram.

"Leave this country and your relatives.
Come with me to a new land that I will show
you. You will become the beginning of a great
nation," said God.

God also said to Abram:

"If you will do as I have asked, I will care for you and bless you. Through your nation of people, I will bring a special gift to all the world."

Abram thought about the words that God spoke to him. He had no children. How would he become a great nation? He wondered where God would lead him. The journey would be difficult to make. The herds, the servants, and all of his possessions must go with him. He would feel sad to leave his home.

But God had spoken. Abram trusted and believed in God. Abram listened to God and decided to obey his wishes.

So Abram with Sarai, his wife, and all his family started north on the long trip toward Canaan. The heavily loaded donkeys plodded slowly along the caravan road. Servant herdsmen drove the flocks of animals.

Along the way they stopped for grass and water for the flocks and herds. At the camping places the women set up the tents of black goat's hair.

The handwoven goat's hair made good tents. When the rains came, the hair would shrink and keep the water from falling inside. To set up the tents, the women would spread the long pieces of goat's cloth on the ground. Then they would get under the cloth and lift it into place with poles. Each tent usually had nine poles with three in each row. Ropes held the tent in place. They were attached to the ground with wooden pegs.

Along the river road they found plenty of food and water. But the trip was hard and long.

After traveling many days, they came to the beautiful and rich plains of Haran. This city was about 600 miles away from Ur.

"Stop and set up the tents," said Terah, Abram's father. "We will live here a while."

In Haran, Terah, Abram's father, died. Nahor, his brother made a permanent home for his family. But Abram did not stay. For God spoke again to Abram.

God said to Abram, "Move from this country and from your father's house into a land that I will show you."

Again Abram left his home to go to Canaan. He took Sarai, his wife, Lot, and all of his servants.

Traveling toward the west and south about 400 miles, they came at last to the land called Canaan. In the distance they saw Mount Ebal and Mount Gerizim. Between the mountains was a pleasant valley with springs of water and woods. Here the tired travelers camped near the city of Shechem.

God appeared to Abram.

"This is the land that I will give your children and their children's children."

Abram loved God. He was thankful for his gifts and his help. With stones he built an altar. At the altar, Abram felt God's presence. He knew God was keeping his promises to him.

Always on the move, Abram traveled from Shechem in the mountain pass to another mountain near the city of Bethel. He set up his tents so that the family could eat and rest. The cattle, sheep, and goats would have grass and water.

Abram was thinking about God. He built an altar by piling stones together. At the altar, Abram talked with God. He asked for guidance and felt God near to him.

"Pack up the tents. Gather the herds and flocks." Abram instructed his servants and family. "We will move to the south."

In the southern part of Canaan called the Negeb, Abram found that the rains had not come for the grass and crops. Food was scarce. There was little grass and water for the herds. A famine was in the land.

The time came when Abram could not find food for his family. He left Canaan and went to Egypt, another country close by. There he found food and all the things his family needed.

Abram was a good and wise man, but he did

not always do right. When he arrived in Egypt, Abram felt afraid. He knew the Egyptians would see his beautiful wife, Sarai.

"They will kill me," he thought, "so that they can take my wife."

With these thoughts in his mind, he decided upon a plan. When the Egyptians asked about Sarai, Abram answered with a lie.

"She is my sister," he said.

Pharaoh, the ruler of Egypt, took Sarai to his palace to be his wife. To Abram he gave rich gifts of sheep, oxen, servants, and camels.

But God was there to forgive and to help Abram. He punished the household of Pharaoh with diseases. Pharaoh became distressed. He found Abram had told him an untruth about Sarai.

"Why didn't you tell me the truth? Why didn't you tell me that she was your wife?" Pharaoh questioned Abram.

"Take her and leave my land," commanded Pharaoh.

Pharaoh's men sent Abram and his family out of Egypt.

By this time Abram was very rich in herds of animals and gold and silver. Lot also had large numbers of cattle, sheep, oxen, and servants.

The wandering family came again to Bethel, the place where their tents had been at the beginning. The altar was still in place where Abram had built it.

Kneeling at the altar, Abram talked with God. He worshiped him and felt his presence near.

Although Abram had no children, he believed God and his promise to make him the father of a great nation of people.

Abraham was a man of faith.

Thinkback: Think about the answers to these questions about the Bible story:

Who were the members of Abram's family? Make a list of their names.

Look at the map. With your finger trace the trip that Abram took without a map. You will want to find the following places: Ur; Haran; Shechem; Bethel; Egypt; Bethel.

What was homelife like in Abram's day?

Do you think that Abram believed and trusted God? Why?

How did Abram worship God?

• Think about the answers to these questions about yourself:

Imagine you are Abram. What would you have thought and felt if God had asked you to leave your home and go with him to a new land?

How does God help you know what he wants you to do today?

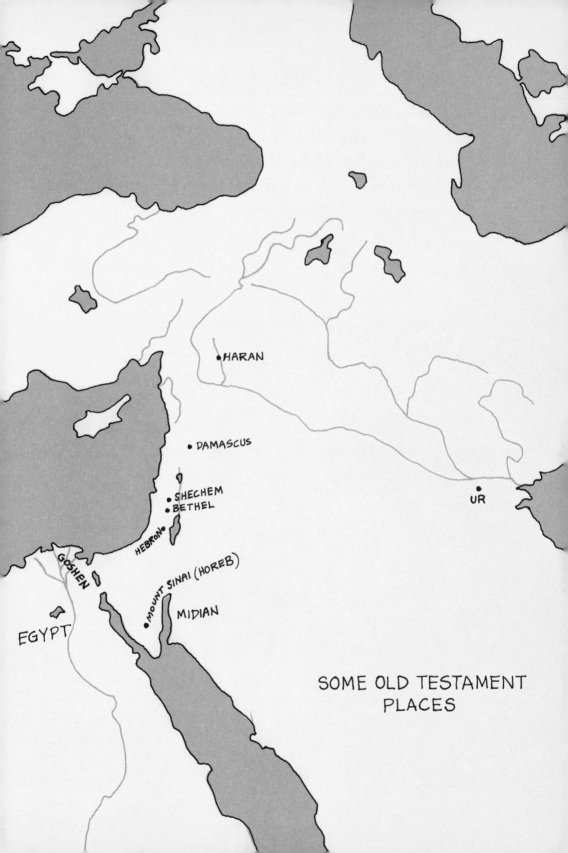

• HARAN

• DAMASCUS

• SHECHEM
• BETHEL
HEBRON•

UR

GOSHEN

MOUNT SINAI (HOREB)

MIDIAN

EGYPT

SOME OLD TESTAMENT
PLACES

A Division Problem

Trouble soon came to the family. Sharp, angry voices of the herdsmen were heard by Abram. His herdsmen and the herdsmen of Lot were fussing over the water holes and the grass of the land.

Abram was disturbed. He hurried to find Lot.

"Lot," said Abram. "I do not want to quarrel. We must not have fussing between your herdsmen and my herdsmen. We are in the same family. I do not want trouble between us. Let us find a way to settle our problem."

Abram took Lot to a place where they could see a long distance. All the land was before them.

"Look around you," Abram said to Lot. "There is enough land for both of us with our flocks and servants. You choose the land in the direction you want to go. I will take the land in the opposite direction. We cannot stay together. The same land will not provide for all of the herdsmen and animals."

Lot looked at the well-watered plains near the Jordan River. Then he looked in the opposite direction at the land of Canaan with its rocky, barren soil.

"I will go toward the Jordan River and the green plains," Lot told his uncle.

So Lot moved his family, his herds, and his servants to the plains near the Jordan River. Lot set up his tents near the city of Sodom.

After Lot had gone, God spoke to Abram. "Look in all directions," said God.

Abram looked to the east, the west, the north and the south of the land of Canaan.

"All this land that you see I will give to you, to your children and their children's children. Through the years, Abram, you will have so many descendents that they will be like the dust of the earth. You cannot count the particles of dust. You will not be able to count your people.

"Get ready," said God. "Walk through the land, and see what I will give you and your people."

Abram heard God. He believed all that he said. As he saw the wonderful land with green valleys and high hills, his feelings were happy and good.

22

At last he came to the plains of Mamre.
Under a large oak tree near Hebron, he set up
his tents. Soon he made an altar of stones.
Abram talked to God and worshiped him.

Abram believed that God would allow him
to begin a new nation of people. But he and
Sarai had no children.

How could there be a nation of people?

23

Thinkback: Think about the answers to these questions about the Bible story:

Why did Abram and Lot have problems?

What did Abram do to solve the problems?

Do you feel that Abram was unselfish?

• Think about the answers to these questions about yourself:

What did you learn from Abram about how to solve a problem?

Have you ever had a problem with someone else?

How did you solve the problem?

Do you know some Bible verses that would help you know how God wants you to solve problems? Read in your Bible the following verses:

Deuteronomy 6:18

Mark 9:50

Luke 6:31

Romans 12:21

Matthew 5:9

Keeping a Promise

Many years had passed since Abram and Sarai had moved to Canaan. Abram had worked hard. He had believed in God and trusted him.

But Abram was worried. How could God make him a great nation of people? He did not have even one child.

Abram talked with God about the promises.

"Lord, what will you give me? Sarai and I do not have a child. Is someone else in my family to be my heir?"

"Do not worry," God told Abram. "I will take care of you. You will have a son. Sarai will be his mother."

God led Abram from his tent. Outside the night was dark. The sky was filled with brilliant stars.

"Look at the sky, Abram," God said. "Can you count the stars? You will have many children and grandchildren and their children's children. They will be like the stars. You cannot count all of them."

"Remember, I am God who brought you out of Ur to this new land of Canaan. I will give you the land. I will keep my promise."

Although Abram had no children, he believed God. God was pleased. He counted Abram as one who was right and good in his sight.

Sometimes Abram was still discouraged. So many years had passed since he had been in Canaan. He was ninety-nine years old. Sarai was growing old too. How could God send a son to them?

One day Abram heard a familiar voice.

"Abram," the voice said. "I am God. Do the right things and try to be perfect."

Abram knew God's voice. He fell on his face and listened to him.

"My promise is still with you," God said. "I wish to change your name. Abram, exalted father, will no longer be your name. Your new name will be Abraham, father of many nations. Your descendants will become the beginning of not one nation, but many nations."

"Do not call your wife by the name Sarai. Her name will be changed to Sarah. She will be mother of many nations."

"In the years to come, your family will grow in numbers. Some will even be kings. And I will be their God."

Something happened one day as the heat of the sun beat down upon the tent under the trees at Mamre. At noontime, Abraham had lifted the flap of the tent and was sitting in the doorway.

When he looked up, he saw three men coming toward the tent. Abraham ran out to meet them. Very politely he bowed toward the ground to greet his visitors.

"My Lord, come under the trees to rest. I will have water brought so that you may wash your feet and rest yourselves.

"I will get food for you to eat."

"Thank you. We will do as you have said," answered the strangers.

Abraham hurried into the tent to Sarah.

"Quickly, make bread upon the hearth for our guests. I will prepare a tender calf for meat."

Soon Abraham gave the guests a meal of meat, bread, milk, and butter. He stood by them under the tree to serve them while they ate.

"Where is Sarah, your wife?" they asked.

"She is in there," Abraham responded as he waved his hand toward the tent.

"Your wife, Sarah, will have a child, a son."

Sarah laughed aloud. She was standing in the tent door and heard what the stranger said.

32

Sarah and Abraham were both old. She did not believe that they would have a child.

But God spoke through one of the men who was visiting that day.

"There is nothing too hard or too great for God to do. This time next year Sarah and Abraham will have a son."

Truly, the good news happened that God had sent the visitors to announce. Sarah did have a son. She called his name Isaac which means "laughter."

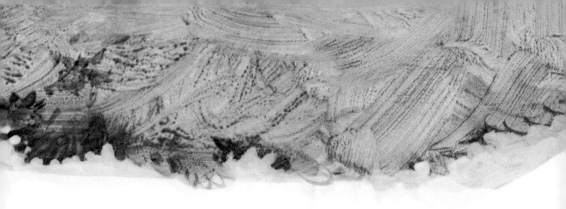

Thinkback: Think about the answers to these questions about the Bible story:

Why was Abram worried because he did not have a son?

What did God tell Abram about the stars and his descendants?

How many visitors came to see Abram?

How did he treat them?

What good news did they bring to Abram and Sarai?

What new names did God give to Abram and Sarai?

• Think about the answers to these questions about yourself:

Do you feel that God tested Abraham's faith in him?

Do you think that God wants you to have faith and belief in him? Do you have?

Just the Beginning

How happy Abraham's home was! Sarah was filled with joy because God had given her a son whose name was Isaac.

Isaac grew. When he was a young boy about two years of age, Abraham prepared a great feast. Everyone was invited to eat delicious foods. They had a happy, merry time thinking about the future days for the boy, Isaac.

Time seemed to pass quickly. Abraham watched his son, Isaac, grow. He taught him much about the herds and flocks. He shared his faith about God and the promises that were made to him through the years. Isaac knew he was an important part of the nation God would build. Abraham helped his son to feel pride for the nation he would be a part of.

Many years passed. Abraham was growing old. Isaac was now a man. Abraham's wife and Isaac's mother was no longer living. The home was not the same without Sarah. Isaac was often sad and lonely.

One day Abraham called his faithful servant to him.

"Eliezer, I want you to go on an important trip. My son, Isaac, must have a wife. I do not want him to marry a woman in this land of Canaan."

Eliezer listened as his master spoke.

"I want you to go to Haran, where my brother, Nahor, and his family live. There you must find a wife for Isaac. She must be from my own kinfolks."

Eliezer knew his master was sending him on a special mission. What if he could not find the right woman? What if she would not come back to Mamre?

With servants and ten camels loaded with gifts, Eliezer set out on his journey. Several days passed before he reached Haran. Eliezer wanted to do well on his mission. He knew that Abraham trusted him.

Eliezer arrived at sundown by the well outside the city of Haran. He waited because he knew the women of the city would come to the well for water.

Eliezer prayed.

"Oh, God, let the woman who should be the wife of Abraham's son come to the well. Let the one who gives me a drink of water and draws water for my camels be the right one."

As Eliezer finished speaking, Rebekah, a beautiful young woman, came to the well to get water for her family.

"Give me a drink of water," the servant asked.

"Drink, my Lord," she replied. "I will draw water from the well for your camels to drink."

Eliezer knew that Rebekah was the young woman that God had chosen.

He learned that she was of the house of Nahor. He gave her gifts of gold earrings and two gold bracelets.

Rebekah took Eliezer, his servants, and the camels to her house.

Eliezer told Rebekah's family all that he had done. He asked them for Rebekah to be the wife of Abraham's son.

Rebekah returned with Eliezer to the land of Canaan.

When they arrived at Mamre, Rebekah saw

a man walking in the fields.

"Who is the man that comes to meet us?"
she asked.

"He is Isaac, Abraham's son," Eliezer told
her.

When Isaac saw Rebekah, he loved her. She
became his wife. Sarah's tent was her new
home. Abraham felt happy and pleased to
have Rebekah in his tent home.

Abraham lived to be the grandfather of twin sons, Esau and Jacob. The boys were fifteen years old when Abraham died.

Through all the years, Abraham had followed God. A new nation of people would come from the family of Abraham. This would be called the Hebrew nation.

The Bible is written about the people of Abraham. Their lives have helped all people to know about God and his plans.

About 2,000 years after Abraham's family left Ur, God sent his Son, Jesus, to the world. He was born to Mary, a Hebrew from the new nation.

God had kept his promise to Abraham. For God had said, "You, Abraham, will begin a great nation. Through this nation, all the world will be blessed."

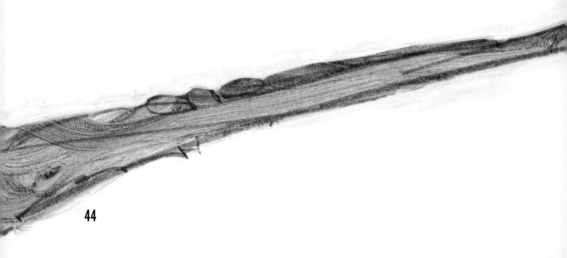

Thinkback: Think about the answers to these questions about the Bible story:

What was the name of the son of Abraham and Sarah?

Who was Abraham's special servant?

On what mission did he send the servant?

What nation did Abraham and his people become?

Who came to bless the world through this nation of people?

• Think about the answers to these questions about yourself:

Do you feel that God will keep his promises to you today as he kept them to Abraham?

Do you know some Bible verses that would help you know why God sent Jesus to the world? Read in your Bible the following verses:

John 3:16
Romans 6:23
Acts 16:31

Reflections

- *Who?*

Who called Abraham and asked him to leave his home in Ur?

Who was Abraham's father?

Who was Abraham's wife?

Who was the son of Abraham and Sarah?

Who chose the best land for his herds and flocks?

Who were Abraham's grandsons?

- *What?*

What did Abraham do to worship God when he reached Canaan?

What important mission did Abraham send his servant to do?

What nation of people did Abraham's descendants become?

• Why?

Why did God call Abraham to start a new nation?

Why did Abraham believe God and his promises?

Why was all the world blessed by Jesus's coming?

All the story of Abraham cannot be told in this book. You may wish to read the whole story from your Bible. Begin reading at Genesis 11:26 and read through Genesis 25.

Date Due

BROADMAN
B|P
SUPPLIES

MAY 1 0 '92			

Code 4386-04, CLS-4, Broadman Supplies, Nashville, Tenn., Printed in U.S.A.